LEADING YOUTH IN SUSTAINABLE DEVELOPMENT

A HANDBOOK FOR YOUTH LEADERS & ADVOCATES

LEADING YOUTH IN SUSTAINABLE DEVELOPMENT

A HANDBOOK FOR YOUTH LEADERS & ADVOCATES

EMMANUEL CLIFFORD GYETUAH

WITH ENAM AMI AGBOZO

The views expressed in this book are those of the author and do not necessarily reflect the opinions of Youth Advocates Ghana (YAG) and the African Youth SDGs Summit Secretariat.

Table of Contents

Foreword

In response to the need to consolidate the efforts and contributions of young people and to offer space for youth participation in the implementation and monitoring of the Sustainable Development Goals (SDGs), we at Youth Advocates Ghana (YAG) established the African Youth SDGs Summit of which I am the convener. Launched in 2017, the African Youth SDGs Summit was the first continental SDG platform led by young people and held in Sub-Saharan Africa as the largest gathering space for dialogue, networking, learning, celebration of successes and participation of young people in the implementation of the 2030 Agenda for Sustainable Development and the AU Agenda 2063.

One of the most important observations through the previous African Youth SDGs Summits was the notable depth of energy, innovation and creativity among the youth.

However, there are gaps in the area of putting ideas and innovations into action and make it a reality.

Leading Youth in Sustainable Development: A Handbook for Youth Leaders and Advocates is the perfect book for any young person in Africa and beyond. Emmanuel Clifford Gyetuah presents the practical steps for you from planning to implementation and sustaining your idea or initiative. I think this book is timely as we enter into the Decade of Action of the implementation of the SDGs.

Unlike many global platforms, the African Youth SDGs Summit prides itself as a platform fully led by young people and I'm very excited that my colleague, Emmanuel Clifford Gyetuah has taken the pain to put this handbook together taping into the experiences we have gathered through the hosting of the Summits and other projects we have implemented at Youth Advocates Ghana. I encourage all young people to translate the insights from this handbook into collective action at all levels.

With about 10 years to 2030, it is important for all stakeholders working within the SDG framework to accelerate their efforts, including strengthening the capacity of the youth to ensuring that no one is left behind.

Emmanuel Ametepey
Executive Director, Youth Advocates Ghana &
Convener, African Youth SDGs Summit

What Youth Leaders Are Saying About This Handbook

As a Student Leader, I have found this Handbook to be very resourceful. Now I have a guide to help me work on my not-for-profit ideas related to the SDGs in order to transform my community and the society at large – **Maame Ama Pomaah Appiah-Adjei,** *Vice President, Ghana Students' Accountability Network (GSAN)*

Now is the time to galvanize and bring young people together towards taking consistent action in advancing the Sustainable Development Goals. I strongly recommend this book for any young person working to advance the SDGs and launching into the development space. It's a good read - **Hammed Kayode Alabi**, *SDGs Youth Champion*

As a practitioner and avid supporter of the Sustainable Development Goals and Global Citizenship Education, I would advise anyone who is looking for support to move from idea to action to read this book. With so many complex challenges failing societies across the world, this book comes at an ideal time to encourage sustainable action - **Stephanie Kirwan**, *Adult & Community Education Practitioner*

Emmanuel Clifford Gyetuah is a different class of youth leader who knows how it feels to be hungry, broke and unknown to any influential person yet have been working towards the UN Sustainable Development Goals. This is a must-read book for every youth leader who may have numerous excuses to give up because she or he is starting from zero - **Kwesi Boadu Ntiamoah**, *Environment & Biodiversity Researcher*

A great handbook for youth looking to make a difference! Rich in content and drawing from real-world experience, this book gives practical and actionable steps to start creating change. Highly recommended - **Marta Verani**, *International Development Professional & Youth Advocate*

Youth tend to be among the first to embrace new ideas and innovations. How do we advance this capacity? My friend and colleague Clifford, a valuable resource person for referrals and best practices answered the question in this handbook. Remember, Readers are Leaders - **Noudéhouénou Marcellin Gandonou** - *Research Associate, UNFCCC RCC Lomé_*

This handbook offers invaluable information for today's budding young advocates. Leveraging on rich personal experiences with Youth Advocates Ghana and real-life case studies from the African Youth SDGs Summit, this book provides its readers with solid evidence and technical guidance on the best practices towards success as a young SDG champion. – **Enu Beula Otsyina**, *Gender and Reproductive Health Enthusiast*

The success of Sustainable Development plans requires multi-stakeholder engagements and Inter-Generational Co-leadership. Most importantly informed literate youths to drive the process are eminent beyond comparison. The information contained in this book is no doubt a necessity for every young African to learn from the practical steps provided by the author's experience in the development sector - **Damilare Oyedele**, *Co-Founder & Chief Executive: Library Aid Africa*

If you are a young person with a strong drive and zeal to lead the positive development of your respective communities and countries, then this is a must-read book. Clifford shares with us a systematic approach on how to go about this using his own life experiences and this is something that makes this book unique. A decade of Action and we are all involved – **Kanubala D. Deborah**, *Machine Learning Researcher*

I started as a youth leader inspired and motivated to lead the way; however, the journey was full of deep holes and mountains. If I had this book then, I would have got here earlier. I needed to learn from the experience of others, not mine - **William Turckson**, *Founder, Brain-nest*

Recognizing the important role of youth in the implementation of the SDGs, Emmanuel Clifford Gyetuah – a young leader with great promise – makes use of his experience of how young people can become actors of change. If you have visions for a sustainable future, this guide will help you transform your ideas into action - **Moa Larsson**, *MSc in International Development and Management, Lund University*

This guidebook is for all youth looking to get into a leadership position. The author shares valuable information you won't find elsewhere- from rounding stakeholders to one platform to maintaining relationships with them and managing finances prudently, it is all one needs to succeed - **Nana Yaa Korankyewa Ayim**, *SDGs & STEM Advocate*

You will rarely find such an exposition of experience in the space of development passionately and carefully chronicled by a young person, especially with the big picture of what it is we want to do for our world. This is a refreshing reminder and a timely inspiration of the chances and power possessed by young people to make our impact count this decade and beyond. Our connectedness and opportunities this decade know no borders and will our collective penury be if we become passive citizens - **Paulina Adjei,** *Development Practitioner*

As a fellow youth development professional coordinating several not-for-profit programmes and working with different organizations, I cannot emphasize enough the importance of having such a hands-on book to assist us especially beginners in this field and therefore highly recommend that individuals as well as organizations patronize it as a very resourceful material and a guide to advance youth development work at all levels - **Ellen Lindsey**, *Climate Action Activist*

It is a passive responsibility on everyone to make a change for a better world. Our ideas need to be put into action by emulating experiences and lessons, and learning from their challenges and errors, those who took the lead before us. I'm by this book curtained for a better world by 2030 as it serves as guidance towards achieving the SDGs for a better world. **- Naa Fofo Djanie,** *Development Communication Specialist & Sustainable Farmer*

Overview

We just entered into the Decade of Action in the implementation of the SDGs and this requires that all stakeholders double up actions to ensure that no one is left behind by 2030. I have been fortunate to work alongside a team of motivated young people across Africa on the African Youth SDGs Summit and other SDGs related projects since the goals were adopted in September 2015. Hence, I recognize the resourcefulness and momentum of young people in driving the development of their respective countries. However, there are still gaps when it comes to knowing how and when to put their ideas into actions.

This handbook is a self-help book for fellow young people. I tap into the experiences of my years of work at Youth Advocates Ghana and share practical steps to help put whatever idea any young person may have into actions.

This book is in five chapters with chapter one capturing the founding story of the African Youth SDGs Summit. I also share something on Youth Advocates Ghana, how it started and of course, the leadership of the organization. I then focus on the successes and challenges with the implementation of the African Youth SDGs Summit. This chapter paints a picture to any young person that there are no excuses in working towards the implementation of any social initiative.

In chapter two, I share the practical steps in getting started with an idea or initiative. I give step-by-step approach in setting objectives and goals as well as defining clear engagement modules in order to attract the right people to journey with. I also share how to craft a working budget and a concept note to sell your idea the best way possible. In all these, I picked from the African Youth SDGs Summit experience.

In chapter three, I look at building traction and mobilizing multi-stakeholder support towards an initiative. Partnership is key and the entire SDGs is anchored on multi-stakeholder partnerships. I give some practical steps and avenues for building and sustaining professional partnerships, picking from the African Youth SDGs Summit and how YAG has been going about it.

Chapter four is where I touch on moving the idea into proper implementation. I share the idea of piloting and how we did it at the African Youth SDGs Summit. Critical steps in reporting and evaluation including financial reporting and auditing were central in this chapter. Also, I share information about a very important skill that is dear to me- debt management.

The last chapter looks at fostering continuity and sustaining the initiative. I pointed out people and plans as the key elements of achieving sustainability for any initiative.
It is very important to note that each chapter ends with at least 5 key points readers should always remember. I have made the layout of the entire book very easy to navigate to aid easy reading.

Enjoy the Read.

Emmanuel Clifford Gyetuah © 2020

CHAPTER 1: AFRICAN YOUTH SDGs SUMMIT

*"To say nothing is saying something. You must denounce things you are
against or one might believe that you support things you really do not."*
— Germany Kent

The Founding Story

We started the African Youth SDGs Summit with no money. It
was only an idea we were passionate about and ready to risk
all we had to see it go through. We were able to do all we did
because of the kind of leader we had - Emmanuel Ametepey.
He is the team lead and founder of Youth Advocates Ghana
(YAG), the organisation behind the African Youth SDGs
Summit.

Emmanuel Ametepey wasn't new to starting and sustaining a
project based on passion and commitment. Youth Advocates
Ghana started in a similar manner.

After passing his High School exams and having no money to continue to the University, he opted for a teaching job which turned out to be the birthplace of his advocacy on a large scale. As a teacher, he grew to become the favourite and trusted one the female students could report sexual advances and harassments to. And it was for good reason: because he always came through for them. He confronted where necessary and threatened if it came to it.

Through advocating for the safety of students in his school, he got the idea to develop the advocacy beyond his immediate environment - the school he was teaching in. That is how Youth Advocates Ghana (YAG) started - as a small organisation with a focus on Nsawam.

The sole focus of the new organisation was to bring onboard interested parties and stakeholders to run social campaigns on sexual harassment, child trafficking and other related issues. Subsequently, a few years after starting the organisation and running a few initiatives, Ametepey got international exposure, which allowed the organisation to evolve into a bigger one with a bigger vision. At this juncture, he stopped teaching and registered the organisation in 2011.

Using the connections and network he built over the period, he raised funds both locally and internationally for the projects that Youth Advocates Ghana worked on.

On one such international trip in 2013, he came into contact with African Monitor - a South African based organisation that collates African voices for African development. African Monitor was running the SDGs consultation process (Post 2015 Development Process) and was looking to work with youth organisations to capture the voices of young people to feed into the African Common Position on SDGs for global negotiations. YAG was recommended to African Monitor as the youth organisation to work with to lead the youth consultation on the post-2015 development process in Ghana. Eventually, the funding for this project - Voice Africa's Future became the first major funding that YAG received.

The 2030 Agenda for Sustainable Development was adopted with goals like decent work (SDG8) and quality education (SDG4) being part of the top issues from our consultation in Ghana. The Voice Africa's Future Project continued and this time we were looking at popularizing the 2030 Agenda among young people and getting some feedback on what they thought about the new agenda for sustainable development.

After months and years of work visiting various communities across Ghana, we rounded up the Voice Africa's Future project and submitted the data and our findings to African Monitor. We were, however, encouraged to carry out a citizen's hearing for the communities we visited to share the findings with them and engage on the key issues raised. The findings and the feedback from the Citizens Hearing became the starting point for the African Youth Summit idea. We wanted to create a platform to engage further on the key issues that stood out from our assessments and the Citizens Hearing after the project, which was SDG 8 - Decent Jobs and Economic Growth.

Why a Summit on SDGs?

Choosing the SDGs as a focus point didn't come by accident. YAG started as an advocate for sexual health and subsequently added more areas of advocacy. However, we realised that all the work we've been doing over the years fits into the Sustainable Development Goals. The SDGs are valid until 2030, and with the data our citizen's hearing engagement provided, we realised the best course of action was to toe the line of advocacy for the SDGs, especially amongst the youth.

We envision that in the next 10 years, a lot of focus will be on the SDGs, especially assessment of the impact it has had in Africa from the time of its inception. And we want to help as many of the youth in Africa better understand the goals, the accountability processes and how they can take ownership of its implementation at all levels. Enough to take bold steps to start initiatives in their home country and across Africa that shift the discourse about the SDGs.

A key observation from the Voice Africa Future's project is that most citizens, especially the youth are unaware of the SDGs. They do not know of its existence or what it means for them as youth. It's thus very important that you, as a youth leader reading this Handbook with a level of interest and understanding of the SDGs, will attempt to change this narrative. Pick a focus area and begin pushing it in your community. Start around you and move towards national coverage. All youth in Africa and beyond must know about the SDGs and work towards attaining these goals for our respective countries and the world.

The Success of the African Youth SDGs Summit

Beyond being driven by data gained from our engagement with citizens, a lot of the success of the Summit depended heavily on the YAG team. How we organise ourselves, engage with stakeholders and ensure we organise a program that is well attended and has given birth to an ongoing discourse on the SDGs which is what we want to see in Africa. Our success as a team proceeds from commitment to the cause, willingness to sacrifice our time, ideas and ideals for better ones, and finally a readiness to neglect comfort.

Starting the African Youth Summit as a fairly young organisation came with it's attend ant issues of funding, proper organisation and lots of stress. Without a car, we endured public transport, the heat from the sun and several trips back and forth just to make the summit happen successfully. Waiting to get 100% funding or to buy a car for rounds will have meant the Summit will not have happened in the year it did, we will still be raising funds even now.

It's very important that for whatever initiative you're willing to start and lead in your home country or community, you're ready to be sacrificed on the altar of hard work minus comfort. All conditions will never be right for you to start, so you might as well start that organisation, initiative or partnership that positively impacts the SDGs discourse wherever you find yourself. This handbook is my contribution to help you start work with no excuses!

The African Youth SDGs Summit Project

To make the Summit happen, we tackled it like a project. As every project has phases, we broke our activities down into the four phases that come with projects: *initiation, planning, execution* and *evaluation*. And these stages have always followed each version of the summit we've run since its inception. Without running the summit as a project, we risk failing at it. To improve the success of your idea or initiative, it will benefit you if you break it down into different facets of a project with conceivable timelines. Remember, failing to plan is planning to fail.

The Project Initiation

The initiation of the Summit starts with the drafting of a concept note.
A concept note is a brief proposal which describes a project idea and the objectives to be pursued in that project. You can submit it to funding organisations, albeit without a formal call for funding. It gives the funding organisation a clearer understanding of the project.

Our concept note includes sections such as;

Background: a highlight of the concept of SDGs and how it has fared so far in Africa - challenges, policies, etc. We also include a summary about the Summit in this section.

Overall Goal: a short statement describing what we created the Summit for.

Objectives: clear descriptions of what the Summit aims to achieve.

Thematic Focus & Sub Themes: these addresses the aspects of the SDGs that the Summit will tackle.

Expected Outcomes: description of the expected results after the Summit has run.

Partnerships & Collaborations: here, we highlight our openness to partnerships from all interested organisations whilst listing some of our key partners.

Format: brief description of the various activities that will make up the summit.

Funding: how we intend to fund the summit.

Coordination: this expands on the event itself: venue/date, expected participants, key language, media/publicity, pre/post-event activities, tentative timelines, and a brief about us - the organizers

Conclusion: we bring everything together into a high-level pitch.

After preparing the concept note, our next activity is to share it with our network for input and shaping. This helps us better improve the concept note overall and gives us better parameters for the next stage of the project. By the end of the initiation phase, we know our scope, what results we're expecting from the summit, when it will happen, and what resources (social, human, financial) we will need to pull off a successful summit. We're better prepared to dive into the next stage, which is the planning stage.

Note: The initiation and planning phases may happen concurrently.

The Project Planning

With our concept note shaped up and in hand, we get back to the drawing board to figure out the project, resource, financial, communication and risk plans that we need to run our summit successfully. Typically, we outline the major activities, tasks, the dependencies across both internal and external stakeholders and timeframes for all the scheduled activities/tasks. You can call this the project plan. It becomes an important point of reference throughout the life of the Summit - serving as our source of truth for all subsequent activities, discussions and implementations.

Aside from the project plan, we also prepare our budget, figure out what materials and resources we'll need, and estimate the number of human resources needed for successful implementation of all pre & post-event activities. This is where we're looking at how many volunteers we'll need, vendors for the event, listing out event centres, etc.

The essence of this phase is to give us a blueprint with which to run our activities and also be able to test our results against what we put down from the beginning. Moving on from the planning, we inch towards the implementation and execution of the plan.

The Project Execution

This is where everything we've put on paper comes to live. The activities and tasks leading to the Summit, and the Summit itself all happen in this phase. For a clearer distinction between the parts of execution, we categorise them into pre-event and event execution. The post-event will fall into our evaluation phase.

In executing our plan, we publish our concept note on our websites and across several media channels both for publicity and engagement. We also run more conversations with potential partners, share our budget and discuss how we can work together on the Summit. This process results in several MOUs and agreements with these partner organisations. The process is continuous, even until the day of the event.

Aside from getting buy-in from partnering organisations, we work towards getting buy-in from the youth - after all; the program is for us. We engage the youth on social media through diverse channels, consistent sharing of the vision, and call to actions to get them to take part in the upcoming summit. I get tasked to use my networks built from various engagements and meetings I have attended to reach out to youth leaders across the various African countries and help create an interest in the Summit. Social media engagement continues until long after the event has happened. It's an ongoing loop for engagement and assessment of impact.

In our plan from phase II, we will have created a skeleton of the event, teams needed, etc. This phase is where we start actively putting the team together, based on the different skill sets needed and nationalities amongst others. We assign specific duties, set communication channels up, and discourse happens on the Summit theme and its discussion points.

The team setup becomes a pillar for driving a successful summit. They engage with vendors, book event spaces, follow up on partnership deals, drive publicity about the event and finally on the day of the event, drive registration, moderate sessions, engage on social media, whilst also ensuring the event runs smoothly.

The execution phase is where your idea comes to life, and if you failed to plan, you'll likely have tough challenges on this side. Especially with teams where you don't understand who you need, why you need them and what they will bring on board.
From execution, we come around as a team to evaluate what we have done, achieved and note down things we should work better at.

The Project Evaluation

At this stage, we have run the Summit and we're sitting down to discuss the good, the bad and the difficult. Usually, during the team assignments, we assign someone to handle reporting and learning besides each team member providing their own report on their assignment area. We use a day or two to review all these reports, note down what we did properly, what we failed to excel at and what we should do in the next summit. Our evaluation phase also includes the closure: where we settle our vendors, debtors, suppliers and everyone who had a monetary or physical resource part to play in the Summit. We also send Thank You Notes to partners, speakers and participants.

Running the Summit as a project helps us properly prepare for success. Your initiative, engagement or event around the SDGs can adopt this structure of *initiation*, *planning*, *execution* and *evaluation* to help you track your progress from start to finish. You don't want to create an initiative that dies along the way, and to avoid that, good planning and forecasting before execution and evaluation is necessary.

Successes, Challenges and Lessons Learned

Success is how you define it for your project or initiative. For the African Youth SDGs Summit, the determinants of success for us are:

Content - that participants learn something new

Sharing - that there is knowledge transfer across board - stakeholders/participants

Networking - that there is extensive networking across board both for stakeholders & participants

From our first edition of the Summit, we hit the success metrics fairly well. The first event was overbooked, participants confirmed that content delivery was in line with the theme, there was peer-to-peer sharing, inclusivity for disabled/vulnerable people, and a lot of the youth took part and got to network and interact with each other and the speakers/guests, building fruitful relationships towards future activities.

Our successes however came with challenges. Our major challenges for the first summit in 2017 included:

Reporting: difficulty in choosing the right metrics & stories to explore

Overbooking: our target was 250, but we got over 400 people attending

Refreshment: because of the large numbers, it become insufficient for the numbers we planned for

Politics of Partnerships: choosing the right partners who fit our idea

Volunteer Motivation: satisfying the expectations of our volunteers to get maximum input

All these challenges taught us some lessons about running a youth initiative. We picked a few lessons from our experience organising the first Summit, then to the second. Some of the lessons are.

- A better understanding of partnerships and using it as a strong pillar in working on our initiatives.

- Developing the ability to identify and define the areas which need more focused energy to ensure the whole event runs successfully.

- Learning how to integrate social media and paid ads into the marketing/promotion strategy we use for our event.

- Learning to create guidelines for receiving partnerships whilst attending to the needs of each partner that comes on board.

- Creating guidelines to ensure conformity to the core agenda of the summit.

Overall, we have had our good times and difficult times running the African Youth SDGs Summit. For you wanting to run any social initiative especially around the SDGs, you need to be ready to stay above the fold and stick to your plan if you really want to succeed. However, in doing that, don't forget to take in the lessons and make adjustments as you move ahead.

I've shared with you the founding story of the African Youth SDGs Summit. You've got a clearer understanding of what we did and how we did it. It's now time to pick the information and apply it to your own initiative.
In the subsequent chapters, you will get an appreciation of the nitty-gritty details of getting started and setting yourself up to survive the test of time.

Points to Remember

1. The best place to find inspiration is around you. What issues jump at you, and do you have a way to solve them?

2. When you build a credible brand, it will open doors for you.

3. You don't need monetary capital to start; social capital can equally do the job perfectly!

4. Ideas remain ideas until you build them.

5. Every initiative goes through several processes and a complete lifecycle, be patient!

CHAPTER 2: GETTING STARTED

"The vision must be followed by the venture. It is not enough to stare up the steps-we must step up the stairs."
— **Vance Havner**

Getting started with your initiative requires a lot of boldness. So, congratulations to you for being willing to start - that's what you need to see the vision come alive. With any initiative, the start will be a little rocky, but with some guidance, you can manoeuvre the terrain comfortably. I share with you in this chapter bits and pieces from our own journey to help you get started.

Setting Objectives & Goals

Getting started the right way will be incomplete without setting some goals and objectives. See this as your way of building your vision, target and mission statements. Ask yourself what you want your initiative or organisation to achieve and how you will accomplish it. Here, your vision becomes your goal (s) and your objectives become your mission (how you'll achieve the vision/goals).

To get you started, answer these questions as iteratively as you can:

- What is the opportunity I've identified and what solutions do I have in mind for addressing the opportunities?

- Which of the SDGs will my solution (s) address? You can find a list of the SDGs here: https://sustainabledevelopment.un.org/sdgs

- What will I want my initiative or organisation to achieve in addressing the said SDG?

- Who are the people this SDG affects the most and where are they?

- How will I measure success and ensure sustainability?

Answering these questions will help you set the tone for the initiative or solution you have in mind. It also serves to transfer your idea to a tangible form, which you can now share for partnership with teams and co-founders, etc.

In our case with the African Youth SDGs Summit, our goal is to see youth take ownership and play critical roles in Africa's socio-economic and political systems at all levels.
To help us stay on track with achieving this goal, we broke it down into objectives. Our goal has remained standard throughout the years however, our objectives keep changing with the feedback from each summit.

In 2018, our objectives were to:

- Create and maximize space for the participation of young people in implementing the SDGs.

- Identify gaps and opportunities for the participation and reporting on young people in the Voluntary National Reviews (NVRs) on the SDGs at the High-Level Political Forum (HLPF).

- Facilitate dialogue between African Youth, youth organizations, civil society organizations, national governments and policy makers to enhance accountability and good governance.

- Create a network for youth and other professional participants to share ideas and best practices and also learn from each other.

These objectives differ from the third edition - 2020 objectives, to:

- Improve awareness and knowledge among the youth about the SDGs and their roles in the implementation, review and accountability process.

- Discuss the mechanisms and strategies for localizing the SDGs and ensuring greater ownership by the youth.

- Develop new and strengthen existing youth networks to engage and monitor the implementation of SDGs.

You can see that having a working and defined goal (vision) makes it easier to plan how to arrive at that vision/goal (objectives/mission). This exercise of setting your goals and objectives is as important as execution and going out to get partners. You can start executing without a plan or a clear definition of where you're going, but somewhere along the line, you must learn to create a roadmap. Either than that, you risk fading into oblivion after you hit challenges of debt, lack of funding/partnerships, etc. However, don't place too much emphasis on planning and crafting a roadmap to the detriment of getting on the field and doing the groundwork to make your initiative or organisation thrive.

Defining Engagement Modules

Now that you have a fair idea of what your goal is, what solutions you're creating and which problem you want to solve, it's time to figure out who you can do the journey with. With this, I'm referring to your team, volunteers, partners, funders, and beneficiaries that will collectively make your solution worth it.

The first people you want to engage are team members. "If you want to go fast, go alone, If you want to go far, go together" aptly summarises the importance of getting team members who buy into your idea. Choose people who have the skill sets, network, experience and expertise needed that you lack. That way, you set yourself up to succeed beyond your own efforts.

Think of what basis you'll want to engage the team on: will you pay them? Will you use volunteers to accomplish your initiative? What will be the relationship you'll want to maintain with your team? How will you make them feel a part of the journey, thus jointly owning the idea and executing on it like it's their own baby? These are some questions that can help you determine how to engage the team/volunteers you'll need to achieve your goals and objectives, hence achieving longevity for the SDG solution/initiative you are leading.

Next on your engagement list will be partners and investors/funders. These people will be the fuel that drives your initiative beyond your team's effort. Outline what you'll need from a typical investor and what benefits they'll get from coming on board. Defining this from the beginning saves you the trouble of falling in with the wrong investor/partner crowd.

Decide which partner/investor is best for publicity, financial support, knowledge/expertise support, experience support and other important metrics that collectively will render your initiative a success. Once you have a clear idea why you're engaging a specific partner, you can determine the various ways to reach, engage and sustain the interest of these partner/funding organisations in your initiative.

Remember, you can't be for everyone interested in SDGs. There's always a best fit. An organisation focused on Climate Action (SDG 13) may be reluctant to spend resources on an initiative for Ending Poverty (SDG 1). So, you have to create the right mapping, outline the perks and benefits for each partner/funding organisation and start engaging per your plan.

With the African Youth SDGs Summit, the initial partner we reached out to turned out not to be the final partners who have supported the summit till today. You need to always think of the sustainability of your idea and go with partners that will stick with you for the long term.

Your final call for defining your engagement modules is to define how you'll engage with your beneficiaries. These are the people who will benefit directly from your solution. Our beneficiaries for the African Youth SDGs Summit are youth who are interested in knowing more about how to influence national and sub national policies using the SDGs.

This is the time to create breakdowns of the people you want to engage as beneficiaries - who are they, where do they live, what problem do they have that you're solving, what are the benefits of your solution to them, how can you get them on board, what will be the most appropriate way to reach, engage and keep them connected to the solution (s) you're providing?

Questions like these will cause you to think long and deep, eventually coming up with classifications and engagement tactics that will fit these people. If you haven't stepped out to talk to them yet, this is a good time to speak with the beneficiaries, get a clearer understanding of the feasibility of your solution and their willingness to use the solution you're providing.

People are key to your solution working, so spend as much time as you can to make sure you get the people right. With the right solution and the right people, you can inch towards sustainable success.

Crafting a Working Budget

Your budget determines whether you get support for your initiatives. It doesn't count for you to prepare a budget because you have in mind some big organisations whose support you are banking on. Disappointments easily come in running social initiatives. It's very important to ensure that your budget is the right one and is lean enough for your initiative to run; but large enough for when you want to expand. You also need to customise your budget for the entity you're appealing to for financial aid - if you are seeking aid. Each organisation has their focus and support areas, and without a budget that has shared input - between what they're doing and what you want to do, you're less likely to get support from the organisation.

See it like a Venn Diagram of value. You produce something that has an intersection with your target funding organisation's goals and focus areas, and you get their support.

The essentials to note about creating a budget are:

- Be clear about what you want.

- Don't just focus on figures. E.g. we want USD10, 000.

- Make sure your budget fits into focus areas of the organisation you need funding from.

- Present budget lines that fit into what the organisation has an allowance for (e.g. venue, refreshment, conference fees, etc.).

- Don't just present large sums of money, break it down into specific categories that allow different organisations to support per their strength, resources & focus.

Since you previously crafted the engagement modules for partners or funders, the best time to use that information is in deciding what to put in your budget and who will support your budget. You need to know that most organisations will not support you to make money, buy flashy vehicles, use expensive venues, etc. They will support you to make your initiative work. However, you will need to put in the time, efforts and strength required to ensure that you do the best with what they give you.

When you complete your budget, schedule meetings with key influencers at the organisations to discuss the budget line you want help with. During meetings, explain to the organisation what you want them to assist with, how much it will cost them and what benefits their organisation stands to gain from supporting you.

Every organisation that supports your initiative needs some promise of a benefit; be it brand awareness, exposure, connection with key influencers, government stakeholders, etc. If you're able to define the benefits to the organisation, you're more likely to win their support financially.

A good thing to keep in mind is not to begrudge those who don't support you from the beginning. Some organisations will only come on board once there are other trusted organisations on board. So, whilst defining the partners and funders you'll need, make sure you consider their authority in the industry and how likely their support is to bring others on board.

Crafting the perfect budget isn't the most important thing per se. The essential is bringing the budget to the right people and being willing to go to all lengths to ensure you fund your initiative. If you have ways to raise funds yourself, do so! Create your budget in such a way that you can achieve it yourself if all else fails. Budget wisely and communicate!

The Concept Note - Where It All Comes Together

Your concept note is part of the documents that help your sponsors and partners make sense of your idea. It is what educates them about what they are getting themselves into. As I said earlier, your concept note is a way to expand on your idea and the objectives you will achieve. Your concept note isn't a rough draft explaining your idea; it is your pitch. It's important that you craft it to sell your idea the best way possible. The quality of your concept note determines if you get asked to bring a proposal or even buy the attention of the organisation or individuals you present to.

A concept note can be very simple or complicated. The simplicity or complexity depends on who you are preparing it for. It is better for you to prepare a concept note after you've identified who will read it. That way, you can tailor it to fit their systems or modules.

When we created the first concept note for the African Youth SDGs Summit, the first organisation we showed it to helped us shape it instead of fund it. This was because we realized that the organization has rich experience in project development even though our objectives did not align with their focus. Unless you want a lot of organisations to read your generic concept note and offer you input to shape it, try to identify specific organisations who you know will be interested. Find out what their system dictates and craft a concept note that meets that need.

If you're interested in solving SDG 2 - Zero Hunger, for instance, this could be a good process to follow to craft the best concept note you can:

- Identify the organisations that support SDG 2 initiatives such as FAO, WFP, IFAD, FARA. The internet is one of your best friends in getting this information, apart from your network.

- Research what the organisation you want to approach expects in their concept note.

- Ask yourself essential questions about the project and start writing the answers.

- Compile your answers into the required format for the organisation you're approaching.

- Create a first draft of your concept note, share for feedback and refine it. Be sure to check for grammar, language, clarity and try to eliminate all errors. Only include the most essential information required.

Once your concept note is complete, you can forward it to the organisation. If you need to present it in person, do so. The format in which you submit your concept note depends on the organisation, however, a word document or PDF are safe options. To elicit some emotional response and interest, you can attach pictures, graphs, illustrations, etc that depict what you want to say. Your concept note gives you a foot in the door, so keep it sweet and concise. Let it sell your idea without being overbearing or boring.

If you intend to support your own initiative and think the concept note wouldn't work for you, there's still a way to have your idea clear and easy to reference. You can use the Business Model Canvas and the Impact Model Canvas. Using the two of them can help you clarify what exactly to focus on for starters.

This whole chapter is about getting started, and I want you to start well. I have included the Business Model Canvas and Impact Model Canvas in the resources section of the book. You can print it out and fill it. Better still use the questions in it as a guide to craft your personalised document which will serve as the source of truth for your idea.

Are you ready to get started?

You've got the grounds work out the door. It's time to build some traction and get things moving. If your idea isn't an event, it means it won't happen just once a while, but will be steady. Meaning you have to find ways of maintaining interest over a long period. In the next chapter, I delve more into building traction for your idea. Until now, you've been planning, it's time to get some work done!

Points to Remember

1. You need to ask yourself hard questions about your idea if you want to see it manifest.

2. Always share whatever document you develop with trusted persons and people in your team for feedback before you finally share it widely.

3. Always have an end you're working towards. Without a direction, you will be blown anywhere!

4. Define who you will impact and who will want to partner or sponsor you to create impact.

5. Focus not only on crafting huge budgets, break them into lines that allow sponsors to choose how to support.

6. Your idea's representation can either cost or benefit you. Represent your idea in the most comprehensive and powerful way you can.

CHAPTER 3: BUILDING TRACTION

"No one can whistle a symphony, it takes a whole orchestra to play it."
— H. E Luccock

Without great partnerships, you risk burning out trying to build traction for your idea. If you can't get anyone else aboard your idea, perhaps it's time to rethink it. For an idea focused on the SDGs, you definitely can't work on it all by yourself. You require a community for accountability, support and guidance. Most people have walked that path or at least have a working idea of what walking it should look like. After defining your idea and setting goals, it's time to engage with the stakeholders and partners you defined for your idea.

I'm defining partnerships for this handbook as: *an agreement to do something together that will benefit all involved, bringing results a single partner operating alone could not achieve and reducing duplication of efforts.*

Partnerships for your Idea

The last SDG is Partnership for the Goals; which means at the core of the SDGs and any initiatives that promote them are partnerships. Partnerships can be hard, especially when you feel no one understands the problem like you do. However, your skill set will be limited, your network will only go so far, even your strength can only last for so long. Be open to partnerships both from individuals who join your team and organisations who support or sponsor your initiative.

Good partnerships are the ones in which there is trust: characterised by effective collaborations, support and loyalty. Good partnerships understand the value of each member on the team, sees everyone as equal and makes room to respect the individual differences. When thinking of partners, you need to look out for the best fit for the journey you're on. These are some qualities you can look out for when scouting for partners.

The qualities apply for individuals and organisations:

They respect others: This is important because there will be times when you'll not agree on an issue, so you want a partner who regardless of disagreeing, will respect the decision you've made and provide support for it.

They have complementary skills: Picking partners with the exact skill set as you could cause a lot of tension and conflicts. Especially when you both have strong opinions about the same issue. You can prevent such tensions by picking partners who have skills that fill in on your weak sides. If you're a marketing expert, they're a finance or legal expert. That way your skill sets fit into the various vacuums that you need to fill to enjoy success.

They have integrity: Your partners should be people you trust. If you have even a hint of doubt which you can't explain away, let that person/organisation go. You should be able to trust that the decisions they make will support the objective and not derail it.

They align with your vision and values: Whoever comes on board must believe in what you're doing and see the prospects you see. If the person doesn't buy into your initiative, you're better off looking elsewhere. The dangers of having on board a partner at odds with your vision and values are extensive.

The partners we've worked with for the African Youth SDGs Summit and our other YAG initiatives have always ticked these boxes. We've had to deny partnerships with wealthy sponsors because their vision didn't align with ours. They had the money to support, but they either had a different agenda or were micromanaging every single activity without giving us any freedom, so we declined such partnerships. You should sacrifice money for the survival of your initiative.

Eventually, the partners we committed to for the Summit played a huge role in building traction for the idea. The Summit went into boardrooms and offices that we couldn't have visited ourselves, but which our partners had access to. Your partners will play a huge role in getting others to believe in and support your idea, so choose the right partners.

Partnership Building Models

Knowing the qualities of the partner to look out for helps you choose which kinds of partners will fit. However, there's a need to go further and drill down into whether the partner is worth going with. Not all organisations or individuals who have the qualities of great potential partners will be the right fit for your initiative. There are those who will align better than others. To help with that, you can use this 4Ps Model to judge the right partner. The 4Ps are *Purpose, Potential, Projections & Practicality*.

Purpose

For each of the partners in your partner pool, identify the reason you want a partnership with them. Is it for visibility, positive branding, 'political' benefits, access to new markets, money, etc.? Be clear on what your needs are and how the potential partner can fill in the gaps. This will help you weed out the ones that shouldn't be partners at all. If you can't find a compelling purpose for the partnership, then perhaps, you shouldn't chase it.

Potential

Now that you know what purpose the partnership is for; you need to outline the key factors that affect the prospective partners. Things like their priorities, expectations, what drives them, their experience regarding your idea, useful track records, and any non-negotiables they look out for in partnerships. Doing this exercise helps you identify potential sources of conflict or disagreements of the organisation with your idea. Thus, making it easy for you to go for or shun the partnership.

Projections

Ultimately, any partnership you enter should bring benefits both to you and the partnering organisation or individual. Highlight the benefits, risks and costs of the partnership. Is it possible to achieve the intended purpose? What will it cost to have this partnership? Will it cost your autonomy or control over your project? How does your partnership benefit the organisation? What potential roadblocks do you foresee in the partnership? Answering these questions prepares you for different outcomes. Armed with that information, the likelihood of the partnership or otherwise becomes clearer.

Practicality

With the purpose defined, the potential investigated, and projections made for the partnerships, you need to find out whether the partnership is possible. Here, you'll ask questions like will there be accountability issues? Will it be easy to clarify each party's roles and responsibilities? Can external factors influence the partnership? Is there a clear way to assess the impact & value of the partnership? If you weren't being realistic with the previous Ps, this P brings you back to reality. Away from your grand dreams about how the partnership will go, is it a feasible partnership? Considering all the factors that come to play? This last P can become the concluding judge for you on whether partnership with a particular organisation/individual is worth it.

After performing the 4Ps test for all the partners you've outlined, what you'll have will be the most likely, least likely and incompatible partners. Starting from the most likely list, you can start thinking of how to reach out to the prospective partners and start negotiations and discussions.

Building Partnerships Through Networking

Aside from writing several letters and always knocking on the doors of potential partners, you can foster partner relationships through networking. Networking opportunities are always ripe for you to meet the partner that could transform your whole idea or initiative.

The essence of networking to any growing project or youth engagement initiative is several. Connecting with the right people and building real relationships at events and other meeting avenues comes with benefits like sharing your vision, building partnerships for funding/support, building databases for the organisations in your field, gaining funding for your projects/activities and gaining thought leadership on issues related to your SDG focus area amongst many others.

At YAG, we have our own model for approaching networking. This is how it looks like: attend relevant events where we look out for key people, have engaging conversations and exchange contacts. After the event, we reach out to the person and stay engaged through periodic emails. We don't play with the database of contacts we build. We require each YAG employee to get at least one relevant contact from every event attended. This action allows us to add to our database of contacts regularly.

To ensure there's a fluid relationship between us and our network, we categorize the contacts based on their interests and then choose a day in the month to call, send emails or interact on social media as a way of staying engaged. All these efforts allow us to provide value to our network, which has allowed us to receive value when we need it.

If you've been adamant with networking so far, start going at it more aggressively. Note down where you need to go to meet those who you can provide mutual value to. Once you're clear on your networking goal, attend events selectively, and give yourself a challenge of forming at least one long-lasting relationship.

Forming lasting relationships starts from leaving lasting impressions on the people you meet. Go prepared and ready to share your own experience as you listen to others share their experiences. That way you connect in person before following up with emails or calls. It ceases to be weird when you send emails or call after connecting during your first meeting. Take your networking seriously and you'll open yourself up to opportunities for finding real and lasting partnerships that will serve your project well.

Negotiating Partnership Deals

Even with the right partners, there's a need for clear understanding of each party's role in the agreement. Negotiating the roles can be difficult especially when dealing with organisations or individuals who are bigger and renowned. There are however ways of aligning such that both parties get the best from the partnership.

The first thing to keep in mind when negotiating a deal with a potential partner is that there's no winner or loser, there are only mutual beneficiaries. Your partnership negotiations shouldn't put you on the winning side, whilst your partners pick up the pieces. Neither should your partners dominate the project to your detriment. There has to be a middle ground that you both come to.

One of our Summit partners from the beginning didn't give us money even though that's what we wanted from them. However, they gave us their name and endorsed our idea. A win for us would have been getting funding, but this compromise of getting their name and support has proven even much more vital to the survival of our initiative. That deal went well because they got a vehicle to drive some of their initiatives, whilst we got their support and endorsement. It was a win-win affair.

Second thing for negotiating a partnership deal is to know when to choose a *collaborative relationship* over a *transactional relationship* and vice versa. In a **transactional relationship**, you choose what you do, what the partner contributes, set fixed expectations for what each party brings on board and rarely discuss any underlying interests.

Transactional relationships will work for partnerships with vendors, suppliers, etc. It can be a long-term relationship, but it never goes beyond the transactions. With the African Youth SDGs Summit, a partnership based on transactional relationships will be what we have with vendors like caterers, owners of venues, printing companies that print our marketing material, etc. The relationship between us thrives on fixed expectations and delivery, with no other underlying interests. However, we pick people we can trust, who have integrity and who understand the importance of having a successful event.

A **collaborative relationship** is one in which you co-create programmes, activities, etc that fall in line with your idea/initiative. In this relationship, you each bring different resources together and share it to achieve success. There are constant discussions, transparency in deciding and adapting to unexpected situations together. These partnerships will be the kind you will have with sponsors and supporters of the initiative. Using examples from our partnerships for the African Youth SDGs Summit, the kinds of partners we have this kind of relationship with are the ones who pay for the cost of the event, supply us with speakers, allow us to tap into their networks, provide capacity building for our team and volunteers, help us shape our programmes, provide guidance and support to the secretariat for ensuring successful events over the years.

These two relationships are essential in building your partnerships and you need to always be on the lookout not to give the wrong relationship to the right partner. Carefully refer to your outline of what needs each partner will meet and clarify the terms from the very beginning. This doesn't mean you shouldn't be flexible. As a youth passionate about the SDGs or leading some youth initiative, you should always be on the lookout for the opportunity to move towards either relationship based on what you're handed with. You can easily convert a collaborative partner into a transactional partner and vice versa.

Lastly, put your terms into a document that you can easily reference. We can forget words easily, documents however last forever. To ensure accountability, it is good practice to record the details of the deal.

Pitfalls to Avoid when Partnering with big Organizations

Getting into partnerships with organisations or individuals who are bigger than you can be challenging. You need adequate preparation so you avoid mistakes that will cost you in the future. With big organisations come tough diplomatic issues to tackle. Look out to avoid these pitfalls when partnering with a powerful organisation:

"Over-promising" - your character & reputation is more important than one partnership deal. Don't over-promise just to get a yes from the partner.

"Over-trusting" - no matter how much you trust your partner, go in with some form of protection. Especially for Intellectual Property and novel ideas/ projects.

Ignoring future impact - if you're thinking of building a long-term project, you need to weigh the terms of the partnership deal, so you don't implicate your project/initiative.

Partnering just for the sake of it - your goal for a partnership is to be effective, not just to have an association with a named partner. The partnership should bring gains to both parties.

Having only one point of contact - your initial contact for the partnership could leave the organisation. Make sure you have contacts of at least 3 others besides your main contact.

Lacking a written and signed agreement - get a lawyer or someone with legal background to draft a comprehensive agreement document which you and your partner will sign. This should include exit/out procedures and conditions. Most often big organizations allow their legal department to put a draft agreement together for your review. When you get the documents, always share it with your lawyer. If you do not have a lawyer, find someone with a legal background to assist you in reviewing it.

Engaging the Beneficiaries of your Project

So far, we've been speaking about the partners. However, another essential aspect of building traction for your project is getting the support of your project beneficiaries. Without them, your partners will support an empty project.

Your beneficiaries are those who you are solving for. For instance, a project on SDG 8 - Decent Work & Economic Growth can have beneficiaries as youth who are Not in Education, Employment or Training (NEET).

With a clear understanding of who you are after, you can build engagement modules that allow you to create the best solutions for your beneficiaries, which usually results in you getting great partnerships. Because, most partners aside from wanting to support projects that align with their primary focus also want to invest in projects that solve problems in a fool-proof way.

Simple ways to engage your beneficiaries

Building a working communication module: break down the communication channels available, map each channel to the people who use it, and then use the information to build an inclusive communication plan that allows you to reach all your beneficiaries, leaving none behind. E.g in most rural communities, your best bet is the information centre or the chief's palace, but for the urban centers, conferences or social media does the trick.

Dig deeper: apart from the problems you perceive exist, speak with the beneficiaries to get insights into some problems you may have overlooked. This way, you meet both the spoken and unspoken needs of the people you're solving for. This makes you more valuable to the beneficiaries and your partners.

Focus on quality rather than quantity: getting the numbers isn't as important as solving the problem at hand. Even if you get to engage deeply with only a few 10s of people out a 100, you have made good progress.

Keep them engaged: solving a problem doesn't make you better or smarter than the people. Stay engaged with them through the most effective communication channel you identified. Whether it's social media, websites, information centres, community centres, etc. Reach your people where it matters the most to them.

Engaged beneficiaries improve the quality of your project. You get constant feedback that allows you to tweak your solutions to fit the rising needs. It helps you stay flexible. Ignoring them because you think you're an expert comes with the danger of fatally failing at the project.

With the African Youth SDGs Summit and other YAG projects, we find the appropriate channels to connect with beneficiaries. Through WhatsApp chat groups, telegram group chats and other social media platforms, we stay engaged and receive constant feedback and inputs during planning, execution and evaluation. You can't help people who are refusing your help or aren't open to the help you're providing. Your people make your success, stay engaged with them at all costs!

Plan an Initiative that Succeeds

After putting in the work to source and build working partnerships and keeping your beneficiaries engaged, the planning of the real work has to start. Your planning will cover recruitment activities, resources assessment, project milestones, success factors, meeting partner agreement requirements, etc. But to do this fixedly, you need a clear picture of what success looks like. Define success on your own terms and work backwards towards the resources and milestones needed to achieve it.

Your success factors can include participation numbers, coverage areas, the number of project beneficiaries, etc. Picking from the African Youth SDGs Summit, we base our success on content delivery, knowledge sharing, networking and participation numbers. Choose the definition of success that works best for your project per the unique constraints you need to deal with.

Move on to resource assessment once you've figured out what success looks like for you. Assess your human, financial, and physical resources. Stack up the available against the required and work towards filling the gap. Determine how many people you'll need on the team and how they'll contribute to success, and how much financial resources you will need to commit at each stage of the project to ensure the success you've envisioned.

Next up is choosing your success team. Your team is equally as important as your beneficiaries and partners. They need to be people who see the need for your project and will commit their time, expertise and experience to making sure it becomes successful. The team is coming to help you attain the success you've envisioned, although you can leave room for new inputs on achieving success.

Since you've already identified partners who will fill the financial resources gap and now have your team handy, you can set project milestones. The milestones will be checkers to show you how far in the journey you've come and how much more you have to go. Setting achievable and timely milestones creates a culture of achievement with your team, which increases momentum and steadily moves you towards your definition of success.

Points to Remember

1. Great partnerships are accelerators for building traction for your project/initiative.

2. Networking is a great way to build relationships that you can convert into solid partnerships.

3. Partnerships with big organisations can be dicey, beware of the pitfalls of "over-promising", "over-trusting", lacking written/signed documents, ignoring future impact, and partnerships just for the sake of it.

4. You can't run a successful project without engaging your beneficiaries.

5. For your project to succeed, you need to plan for success.

CHAPTER 4: MOVING INTO IMPLEMENTATION

"Be creative while inventing ideas but be disciplined while implementing them."
— Amit Kalantri

In the past three chapters, we've been looking at getting off the ground with your project, idea or initiative. In this chapter, we want to look at the implementation of all the plans you have made. Implementation of your project starts with recruitment of your team, signing MOUs with partners, vendors, suppliers, etc. and finally piloting the project, evaluating the results from the pilot and dealing with debts or pressures that may arise.

Recruiting Your Team

Today, there are a lot of opportunities provided by digital technology to help you reach out to and connect with like-minded people all over the world. In recruiting your team, you can start from your personal network - both offline & online. Reach out to trusted friends, acquaintances and family who will have an interest in what you're doing. Social media, in-person visits or phone calls works.

If none of the people in your network can take on the challenge, you can open it up to other youth on social media. Send personal messages to those whose profiles fit your goals or provide direct access for them to contact you if interested. You can also create a Google Form that outlines the information you need to assess the person and provide as much information as possible about the initiative. Fortunately, all these activities will cost you nothing at all.

When sourcing candidates for your team, remember your stature as a non-profit and make this stance very clear to everyone who wants to join. Your best bet will be on people who understand the implications of being a non-profit monetarily yet comprehend the impact of the project you intend to work on. Once you're able to identify such people, you can begin further discussions based on their roles and the compensation packages you have for them, if any. The quality of your team will affect the speed at which your initiative prospers and achieves impact. The wrong people will delay you unduly, the right people will accelerate you to success.

To keep your team members in sync, you can provide an engagement letter outlining the relationship between you and what you expect from them. Adding a project plan that details the life cycle of the project, with specific highlights of their role is also in place for effective work.

Once you're set up with your team, you can move on to tackle your partnerships, vendors and supplier relationships and agreements.

Signing MOUs

A memorandum of understanding (MOU) is a written agreement between two organizations or parties that help establish the ground rules for any partnership activities you explore. It is a tool to facilitate partnership and ensure a smooth working relationship between you and your partners.

All the work you did in mapping out partners, vendors, suppliers, etc that fit your specific needs will prove useful in this stage. This is the stage where you are concluding your agreements with your partners, vendors and suppliers.

For the African Youth SDGs Summit, this stage is a very crucial one for us, because it is the time that proves if we have done our homework properly. We usually draft the MOUs, meet with the partners and discuss the terms frequently until we reach a singular agreement.

Your MOU should outline what each party agrees to contribute to the partnership, a timeframe for delivering the desired outcomes, details of exactly how each party will collaborate (e.g., regular in-person meeting, conference calls, written approval of all activities by both parties), and how the parties will authorize and pay for any costs incurred in delivering the desired outcomes. A good practice is to have a legal counsel review the terms for you before you append your signature. An MOU can be a legally binding document.

Features of a complete MOU

Details: there is a clear outline of what specific projects and initiatives you are collaborating on, including the scope and the time of the projects or initiative.

Information: details of how costs associated with joint efforts will be authorized and paid for.

Guidelines: clear definitions of the use of each organization's logo and name in joint materials such as press releases, fact sheets, brochures, websites. For example, do your partners have branding guidelines that you must follow when creating joint materials?

Ownership: Definition of ownership of jointly developed materials and use of those materials after the expiration of the MOU.

Announcements: does your MOU state if and how you will announce the partnership to the public and/or media?

Period of Performance: Your MOU must have the validity period stated. It should include the date the MOU takes effect & when it ends. If there will be a need for renewal, make sure you include the language to allow for renewal of the agreement. Make provisions for impromptu ending of the agreement and what procedures will be necessary to make that happen.

Point of Contact: both parties entering the agreement must have a contact person who will facilitate the collaboration.

Signatures: your MOU isn't valid until the signatures from leadership within your partner organizations and yours are appended. This will be signatures such as that of the executive director, board president, or other designated person. It should also capture the date they sign the MOU.

For your vendors and suppliers, you can also sign an MOU with them, or create an engagement or contract letter that outlines the relationship between the two of you. You can easily take necessary action when one defaults on their side of the agreement.

With formalised partners, vendors & suppliers agreements, you can pilot your project. It's your option to either pilot first or gets partnerships sorted before piloting.

Piloting

Piloting or a pilot is an initial small-scale implementation of your overall project that you use to prove the viability of your project idea/concept. You test the desirability, feasibility and validity of your idea on a small budget.

We started off the African Youth SDGs Summit with a pilot to host at least 250 young people and we planned for it. Even though we got numbers far above our initial budget, piloting allowed us to test the validity of the idea. Giving us room to pivot as the years have gone by.

Before scoping your pilot, take into account the capacity of your team and the people you will implement the solution with. Piloting doesn't mean doing the full scale all at once, it's a mindset of understanding how incremental change can bring you the desired results. To be successful with your pilot, you need to decide what you're testing.

Are you testing the response of your beneficiaries, the impact of your idea, the scale you can reach? You should be clear about exactly what discoveries you want to make about the project you're launching.

With the African Youth SDGs Summit, our pilot was a test of concept to see how many people are interested in the SDGs, how policymakers will respond to the discussions and the quality of the event. At the end of the first edition, we had enough information to validate these pointers. Based on the pointers, we've made changes as the subsequent editions happen.

A launch plan will help you scope your pilot activities and give you a roadmap to follow. If you're piloting for three months, your plan will highlight what will happen daily, weekly and monthly, across the three months. You can review what an example of a launch plan looks like in the resources section.

With a simple pilot plan, you can take off. As you implement, you learn and adapt as situations and circumstances change. The good thing about your launch plan is that it's a guideline, not the compulsory path to take. Be flexible enough to make changes if things don't go as planned. Don't lose faith in the idea because you face challenges. Remember, you're testing the desirability, feasibility and viability, and without your full commitment, you will get the wrong results. Getting the right results requires paying keen attention to the processes, pivoting when necessary and learning all the time.

Evaluation & Reports

Evaluation allows you to assess the effectiveness of your project. It can also highlight whether your project is moving steadily and successfully towards achievements or slacking. Based on what you learn, you can celebrate and build on successes whilst you learn from what has not worked so well.

You can do evaluations as frequently as possible: daily, monthly or quarterly. The frequency depends on what you're doing and what you want to measure. It also depends on what types of partners you have. Some partners require regular reports to know the state of affairs.

With the African Youth SDGs Summit, our major evaluations happen after the summit. However, during the planning, we always ensure that we stay up to date with happenings, identify challenges to be fixed and draft recommendations to help us be better in the next phase of execution. Usually, for our post Summit evaluations, we have a key person responsible for collating the collective reports from various departments and teams. However, each team has a key person responsible for preparing the report for that team which is later integrated into the overall Summit reports.

For every evaluation you undertake for your projects, establish a clear baseline against which you can compare your results. Set up systems to help you gather the data necessary - surveys, interviews, observations, etc. Once you've got the data, interpret and compare it against your baseline to discover where you did well, where you fell short and where there were unexpected learning or successes. You can compile the discoveries into a report that you share with your team and partners for discussion. Evaluations help you catch problems before they become full-blown.

For financial reporting and auditing, you will not be required to report only on the project activities, but also every expense made. Dedicate a member in your team to be responsible for tracking your expenses and keeping records of all expenditure whilst logging receipts. Any partner that will give you money will require that you report back with receipts as evidence of the various expenditures that happened per the indications in your budget. At the end of every year, engage an auditor to help audit your organization or the expenditure of your initiative. Share the audit report from the auditor with your partners. With this, you don't just demonstrate that you are trustworthy, but you also win them over to support you throughout the lifecycle of your project and in effect helping to sustain your initiative.

Debt Management

Debt and pressure have been a part of the journey for us at YAG, especially with relation to the Summit. Being in debt isn't necessarily a virtue we hail especially for new projects. But sometimes you run into debt -not bad debt, mostly good debt.

One reason you could run into debt and have to manage it over time is having to pre-finance a project for your partners. Some partners require you to pre-finance the project and get paid after implementation. Without a plan in place for pre-financing, you can end up losing huge & impactful partnerships. At YAG, we've had to manage some debts over the past few years and fortunately, we've become better at managing it and ensuring we don't lose our vision amid all the debt.

Interestingly enough, such situations have taught us to work on projects on time whilst sticking to quality and on budget. Our plan for pre-financing such projects is to call on our existing vendors and suppliers. We negotiate and make agreements with them that allow us to get access to the goods, services and support we need to start and complete projects to pay later.

Another reason you can run into debt is inaccurate budget projections. This happens because of the lack of in-depth understanding of the cost elements involved in some project terrains. You won't always have it clear, and there are certain projects you may not have worked on before. All these perspectives can make your budget short-sighted, which will affect the amount of money you have to disburse, eventually landing you in debt you didn't plan for.

It will be a great idea to avoid debts, however, it isn't always realistic to wait for money to come before you work. If you can negotiate and build trust with your vendors & suppliers, you can get work done proactively instead of waiting till you have money in hand to start your project.

Dealing with Debt

Be upfront: be honest with your vendors & suppliers about the terms of the agreement for the project. Once some know what you're signing up for and the value for them, they're more open to providing you the goods or services on credit.

Keep the vendors & suppliers in the loop: assure them of their money coming in. It's not time to be missing calls and turning off your phone when you have vendors & suppliers chasing you for their money. Make yourself available to them always - even if they call you incessantly. It is their ability to trust you during these times that give them the courage to trust you again next time.

Dialogue & negotiate: owing someone doesn't mean you can't have meaningful dialogues and negotiations. Engage your vendors & suppliers in healthy dialogues, negotiate for more time, explain delays, etc. Always keep the communication lines open.

Being in debt comes with pressure. And with pressure comes a need to learn how to manage it whilst still being focused on your activities. There will be pressure from the project beneficiaries, partners, funders and especially the creditor. The pressure can sap your energy and drive for what you're doing, but you can rise above it.

What has worked for me (and my colleagues in the team may have different ways of dealing with it) has been:

- Not complaining when the pressure comes. I find my comfort place & stay there -music, food, conversations with colleagues/mentors, etc.

- I prioritize the issues that are coming at me. I figure out which one needs more attention and start from there.

- I multitask. I do two or three things at once. I make use of commutes, lunch breaks, etc. to clear work from my plate. It helps me to reduce the amount of work I need to do later.

- I set reminders to keep me in tune with all I've got to do. The reminders on my phone become my filter from confusion and loss of priority. Even if I forget to do something, the reminders help me remember.

Overall, the skill of managing debt & pressure is important to have, especially for anyone who wants to start a social initiative or be a youth leader. There are times you won't have money to pay for the materials you need for your project, but that doesn't mean you should stop. You need to learn how to negotiate for things on credit, so your work still gets done and you achieve your impact and objectives.

Points to Remember

1. Piloting your idea is a good way to test the validity, feasibility and desirability of your solution.

2. When engaging your team, partners, vendors or suppliers, have a laid down agreement.

3. Evaluations allow you to know how you're doing along your implementation phase. Don't delay it unduly.

4. Keeping financial records is important. Dedicate personnel to it and keep your partners updated about your audit reports.

5. Debt will come along the journey of implementing your project, how you manage it determines if you survive.

6. Working with people, partners & vendors/suppliers means there'll be times of pressure. Learn to keep your head above water regardless of what happens.

CHAPTER 5: FOSTERING CONTINUITY

"To sustain longevity, you have to evolve."
— **Aries Spears**

A successful pilot creates the opportunity for you to establish your project and become sustainable. Building sustainability for your project doesn't come on a silver platter, it takes your dedication and willingness to think beyond today into the future. The key things you can do to achieve sustainability range from having a continuity plan & long-term strategy to teaching others and prepping the next generation to carry on the vision. It also needs you to be very good at predicting what the future holds and preparing yourself to thrive no matter how things turn out.

For most organisations, we limit the focus for continuity and sustainability to the top-level C-Suite executives and managing directors. However, I think there's the need to look beyond the leaders of an initiative to the implementers and the people who believe in the vision. Once you have a whole team of the next generation that truly believes in your vision, they can rise into leaders who drive that vision. If the focus remains only on the leaders, once they leave, the vision may die.

Focusing on the youth arena, the definitions for youth by the United Nations is 15-24 years, whilst the African Union- in the AU Youth Charter, defines youth as 15-35 years. This shows that you can't work in the youth space all your life. There will be a time where you must move on for someone else to step in. It doesn't matter whether you have a youthful mind or heart, once you're past the age, you'll no longer be an active player in the youth space. This makes it more important to put in structures to ensure continuity of the project you're working on.

Fortunately for us working in the youth space, there are a lot of young people who are making themselves available for mentoring. Offering you the opportunity to pick out the best amongst them who you can intentionally transfer your ideas, knowledge and way of doing things to.

My personal story is one of such stories. My boss at Youth Advocates Ghana found me on social media sharing my passionate opinions on youth focused issues and he reached out to work with me. Over the past years, he's given me the opportunity to lead initiatives, take responsibility for brokering partnerships and shadow him at what he does. That is his way of ensuring there's another like him who is passionate about the work and can easily take over when he's ready to leave. It will then be my responsibility to do the same for other young people. Not necessarily in the exact manner, but in my willingness to share, impact, mentor and coach other young people into solving the various issues we face in society.

Having started the African Youth SDGs Summit and being a youth led and youth focused organisation - Youth Advocates Ghana, it has been a key area for us to invest in the next generation.

We've had some progress so far trying out these actions:

- Allowing the interested youth to explore. We don't restrict them to a particular space. The industry is huge, so allowing them to find where to fit in is important.

- Sharing opportunities, ideas & best practices with them to allow them to find their footing.

- Creating coalitions and communities that help the interested youth learn the ropes for pursuing their interests in the youth development and advocacy space. One of such coalitions we created for the African Youth SDGs Summit is the 2030 Youth Alliance.

- Sharing our networks of organisations & partnerships across the continent with the youth organisations that are part of the 2030 Youth Alliance to help them function with support even though they are in contexts different from ours.

- Starting a webinar series focused on helping young people to tap into our experience as youth-led organisations. This provides content and information that is always accessible to the youth who are interested.

- Recommending some youth-led organisations we know for opportunities for funding and partnerships that come up in our network to set them up for success.

Qualities to look out for when choosing the Next Generation

Genuine interest: With an ability to keep the interest sustained regardless of what happens. It has to be an interest that goes beyond making money, becoming famous and gaining material things. It should interest the person to learn and understand how their contributions can make an impact.

Focus & Learnability: Willingness to learn and stay with the field of interest you are in. The person has to come in fully without doubting if they want to stay or go. That's how the person will build genuine and lasting networks and social capital.

Capacity: the person doesn't have to come in at 100% capacity but can build the capacity over time through learning and staying focused on the interest area.

Building a Sustainability Roadmap

Aside from directly pouring into the next generation, having a long-term plan & strategy is important for carrying on the vision. Here are some ways to ensure you have set your organisation up for sustainable success:

Ensure that your leadership and your culture are consistent: your values as a founder permeate the entire organisation. This means your team will watch and do what you do as opposed to what you say. As a leader, you need to live by the standards you set. You don't list out a value such as punctuality and generosity but come in late for every meeting because you're the boss and rarely support the needs of your team despite having the means. If your values align with the organisation's values and your people see you living and defending it all the time, they learn from you and also build that foundation. That way, even after you've left, there's a legacy that carries on across generations -giving your organisation a lifetime that is longer than you.

Engage in resource mapping: you're the only one with an adequate knowledge of your network, partnerships and way of doing things because they proceed from who you are. If you want your organisation to survive you, it's very necessary to map the resources you've built. Map the assets you have, the resources you've built and the communities or focus areas you're serving as an organisation. Bearing in mind that when your organisation loses relevance to your target audience, it faces the risk of dying. A great map of assets against partners, funding, resources and focus areas allows things to move on and your organisation to grow stronger instead of fading out after you've left.

Creating and maintaining a web presence: in today's digital world, being invisible online amounts to losing out on opportunities for collaborations, funding & partnerships. Set your organisation up online. Be it social media or a website, let your presence be felt and make yourself easy to find by people who want to volunteer, support or work with you. Since the internet never forgets, your organisation can continue thriving after you've stepped away.

Create a bigger vision: having worked in a particular area over years makes it possible for you to come up with insights that can affect many more people positively. Your experience creates an opportunity for you to become the go-to person in that focus area, locality or region. This opportunity allows you to make plans to expand and scale beyond your initial beginnings. The African Youth SDGs Summit is known as one of the most viable places to engage youth in the SDGs, which has given us the opportunity to start country-based summits to allow the vision to spread beyond those who can travel to Ghana or any other host country.

A vision of the future based on history is always a good place to leave the next generation to start from. They have history to look to and the future to plan for.

If there's any key idea for you to pick about continuity for your youth led organisation or project, I hope it is that people and plans are the key things for achieving sustainability for your organisation/project. The people you bring on board, train and pour into become those who pick your vision for the future and lend life to it. You won't always be in the youth space; you'll grow and leave the scene. But before it gets to that, make sure you've left a sizable number of successors, not just as leaders but as believers in the vision and you have also cast a vision for the future that they can run with.

Points to Remember

1. The next generation needs to understand the import of the fight you're fighting to carry on.

2. Who you pour yourself into has a huge bearing on how sustainable your organisation becomes after you've left the scene.

3. Choosing the next generation to pour into requires a lot of discernment beyond words and appearances.

4. Your vision for the future is what will give purpose to those who succeed you.

5. Don't leave your people unprepared. Create a roadmap for them that can lead them into the future they expect.

Resources

Visit this address: https://bit.ly/2vTuAWb to access some templates for making your work much more effective! You'll find templates for:

1. Concept Notes

2. Budgets

3. Business Model Canvas

4. Impact Model Canvas

5. Recruitment/Staffing Plan

6. MOU

7. Reporting template